SPINE

OF THE

TEMPLE

SPINE
OF THE
TEMPLE

Effective Methods to Execute
Administrative Excellence in Ministry
and Marketplace

LANA MCSWAIN

Spine of the Temple: Effective Methods to Execute Administrative Excellence in Ministry and Marketplace.

All scripture used is from KJV.

URLs in this book may change.

Printed and distributed in the United States of America.

Author: Lana McSwain

info@spineofthetemple.com
www.spineofthetemple.com

ISBN: 978-0-578-63860-7

BIO

Lana McSwain is a licensed and ordained minister whose assignment is kingdom building through empowerment. Born and raised in a Christian home and church she started working in ministry when she was very young. Many of her leadership roles in ministry, both past and present, include: associate minister, Sunday school superintendent; Bible study instructor and curriculum director; led married couples' ministries in local churches; advisor and mentor for the Christian Mentorship program at the Mt. Pisgah Church; founder of the "Just Us Gurlz" conversation group for pastor's and minister's wives.

She is an honorary member of the Orthodox Woodriver District Baptist Association for minister's wives. Lana McSwain sat under many other great men and women during her career and time in ministry. She worked as program coordinator and administrative assistant for Oprah Radio; executive assistant at Johnson Publishing Company, Mesirow Financial, Merrill Lynch, Accenture and a couple other great companies. In previous years, Lana was privileged to briefly serve the King of Zimbabwe; and have met two U.S. Presidents and a host of celebrity greats.

She was administrator of the Women Empowered by God (WEBG) outreach ministry for nearly 10 years. This was a downtown Chicago outreach geared toward the working class. Currently, she is the executive administrator to the CEO & Sr. Pastor of a mega-church in Chicago.

Lana received her bachelor's degree in Business Administration from Robert Morris University; and is currently enrolled and pursuing her speaker, training certification with the John Maxwell Leadership training school. She was recently recognized for her contributions in society and received the Women in Ministry Award from County President, Toni Preckwinkle.

Lana McSwain is the brand-new author of the book entitled *Spine of the Temple* effective methods to execute administrative excellence in ministry and marketplace.

Lana McSwain has been married to Pastor Anthony McSwain Sr. for nearly 30 years. They live in a suburb of Chicago; they have seven sons and one daughter and 14 grandchildren.

ACKNOWLEDGMENTS

I want to thank my Lord and Savior Jesus Christ for giving me the ability and the wherewithal to do anything that I do. This book was initially inspired by God and I pray that it blesses everyone who reads it.

I want to extend a special thanks to Laverne Thomas. She is a dear friend, author, publisher and business owner who inspired me to write this book during my time of recovering from cancer surgery. Her contributions to my life are invaluable.

To my ministry acquaintances who continued to push and encourage me to move forward and do the unthinkable.

To Willie Halbert one of the most successful, brilliant, accomplished women I know. You and Charles have truly been supportive and encouraging to me and my entire family. Thank you for believing in me.

To my husband, Pastor Anthony McSwain Sr., I want to thank you for being by my side every step of the way. For the encouragement, support and help you give me from day to day. I could not have done this without you.

INTRODUCTION

You may have asked yourself, what is *Spine of the Temple*? Who or what could this book possibly be about? Or may have said, *what a stupid name for a book*. Don't worry, I thought the same thing, so I'm not offended. It's OK. However, I started thinking of what I do and what I have been doing for the last 35 years.

As I think about the profession I've given my life to, I recognize that what I do is vital to the organizations I serve. I also say to myself that I am an important person and my role is important. The impact I have on organizations and its executives, the influence I have on others, and the lasting residue of a successful project completed with little to no hiccups is amazing, to say the least. The reality is that all of this speaks to the necessity of amazing executive assistants, administrators, administrative assistants, receptionists, secretaries, office managers, or simply anyone who can provide phenomenal help.

I graduated from college with a business administration degree not knowing what career opportunities my degree would lead to. I did not know where my degree would lead to nor did I know what I wanted to do. I was constantly looking for my purpose. As I was determining my career path, I took an administrative position to give me time to think about what exactly I wanted to do. Before the entrepreneurial and technology age, many college graduates started out in the administrative/secretarial field as a catalyst to be launched into the next career platform. Administrative work was easy employment to gain, it was available to help you pay the bills, but it was never a position that one would set as a career path.

Being an assistant was (and in some ways still is) considered a very lowly and minimized job as some would say. Even today, sometimes you will find people who refuse to admit that they were once a secretary or an administrative assistant. Those types of positions used to be considered embarrassing positions and they weren't respected. Truthfully, I understand that mindset. Until I matured, I felt like my jobs as a secretary, administrative assistant, and executive assistant were worthless positions to hold. I felt unfortunate that this profession was all I could gainfully be employed as. After my first year of college, I was determined to make money to be able to live on my own and be able to do some of the things I desired, so I took the first opportunity in secretarial work that was offered to me.

I went to secretarial school for starters. I figured this was a way to make quick money while I figured out the rest of my life. Although, I was hoping to find another type of career, I quickly discovered that secretarial/administrative work was beginning to be a great fit for me. I had evolved, enjoying much of what I had learned while being a secretary to many executives. I also recognized that I loved to help others do well. It was natural to me to be an assistant. I gained sincere pleasure out of helping others look good and not get noticed for it.

In an earlier discovery, I found that in my daily in-office mannerisms it was obvious that I could provide the necessary support and never require a formal announcement or platform regarding what form of contributions were made by me. I simply gained pleasure out of helping other. Naturally, there are moments when you want to be recognized for your work, however, over the years I had become immune to not receiving formal acknowledgment of the work that I was doing. Crazy, right?

We live in a society where people who are deemed unimportant, rarely get the credit they deserve – especially in the workplace. However, after experiencing lack of recognition enough times I individually learned not to take it personal. And if you're in the field of the administrative profession, learning this is very critical to your own success.

As I developed and matured in my field, I began to build my confidence in my abilities and skills. Yes, my administrative works are skills that I acquired over the years and have perfected through education, training, on-the-job experience, never let anyone tell you that administrative work is not a skill. Confidence comes with knowing. If you have contributed to corporations like I have over the years, you will come to recognize that what you do is needed and it is necessary, irrespective of what others think, say, or do.

With all that being said, here begins my story. My story is mine and it conveys how I got here and why I have remained. I acquired the value of providing administrative support to executives and their organizations. The significance of what I bring is invaluable. Though it is usually not stated or acknowledged, it is just something you must know regardless.

I want to bring to your attention the historical view of secretaries, administrative assistants, executive assistants, etc. In essence, they are all the same. The titles typically vary depending on the organization and who you support within the organization, industry, the company structure, and what practicums they embrace.

For thousands of years, administrators existed and provided administrative support to the lead/leader, priests, rabbis, manager, supervisor, executives, etc. What intrigues me the most regarding my findings is that the Holy Scriptures (Holy Bible) would not have existed without the blessing of *scribes* who would write, document, and transcribe messages and teachings, rules, governances and lessons that we read today. According to our current dictionaries a *scribe* is "a public clerk or secretary, especially in ancient times. A professional copyist of manuscripts and documents. A person who copies documents, a person who makes handwritten copies before the invention of printing." I can remember taking dictation, shorthand,

and transcribing recorded messages from cassettes. Although, I had a very strong dislike for dictation, it was certainly part of the job and it had to be done.

The above is a mere fraction of what we administrative professionals do, there are so many other aspects of our jobs as administrators/assistants. We have amazing abilities that occasionally exceed many of the people we support. We are multi-taskers and we wear multiple hats. As you will find in the coming chapters, we become everything to everyone. We have to be *know-it-alls*. We must *get it out* before we've *figured it out*. We must *know it* before we are even *told it*. We are expected to do it perfectly without ever having the experience or formal training. Thus, if you are operating in any of the abovementioned capacities, you must know that you are truly and simply amazing. In a lot of cases, your value has not yet been truly and fully recognized. You mean more to the organization and people then they could ever realize. Many of our bosses have literally no clue of the worth you bring to them and to the organization. All of the behind the scenes work that goes into coordinating a meeting, developing communication, defusing conflicts, scheduling, managing them or an event, would not be done if it weren't for you. Your boss has no idea the level of patience and assertiveness it takes to answer a call for them knowing that it is a prank call or an annoying customer, a client or someone you know the boss prefers not to speak with. The methodical, tactful ways you must cover for them without disclosing the real truth behind the *why*, requires skill, practice, technique, and experience.

The absolute bottom line is that life as an administrator/assistant in any organization, be it corporate, not-for-profit, entertainment, etc. is a necessity, and not having adequate or enough support from an assistant would be disastrous. Knowing this will help you to build your confidence and self-worth as an administrative professional. I need for you to know and realize your significance and your value. Even if no one else ever says a word to you about your worth and value, my sister, and/or my brother, be true, authentic to yourself. Remember there is no one like you. No one can do what you do, the way you do it, and most importantly, no one has your why.

Reading this introduction, you may have discovered why this book is entitled, *Spine of the Temple*. And if you have not, I'm going to make it clearer in the next few paragraphs. I will define the *spine* for you, so that you'll be able to make your own comparisons and understand all the vital parts of the spine which will further inform you of whom you really are and why.

THE SPINE

There are five parts of the spine, but I'm going to focus on the four main vital parts of the spine. **Cervical Spine:** protects the brain stem and the spinal cord, supports the skull and allows for a wide range of head movement.

Thoracic Spine: Protects the rib cage and ligaments, and the vital organs.

Lumbar: it is designed to carry most of the body's weight. It allows for significant flexion and extension movement but has limited rotation.

Sacral/Sacrum: connects the spine to the pelvis; fits between the hip bones.

There are three main functions of the spine: (1)

to protect the spinal cord, nerve roots, and several of the body's internal organs; (2) provide structural support and balance to maintain an upright posture; (3) enables flexible motion.

Without the SPINE, there could not be a functioning body. Without an assistant (executive, administrative, secretary, receptionist,) there could not be a properly functioning organization. We have one of the most important roles of any organization.

THE TEMPLE:

The dictionary defines *temple: a building dedicated to religious ceremonies or worship; an edifice or place dedicated to the service or worship of a deity; a church, a large or imposing one. Something regarded as having within it a divine presence; another name for a synagogue; any place or object regarded as a shrine where God makes himself present, the body of a person who has been sanctified or saved by grace.*

Though there are numerous definitions of *temple* from the dictionary, I would like to focus on this one: *a building or place dedicated to the worship of a deity or deities; a building regarded as the focus of an activity, interest, or practice.* Now you can better understand the title of this book, *Spine of the Temple.*

I have had nearly the same number of years in church administration as I have in the corporate world. I have worked both markets simultaneously over the years. Administration in the temple should operate under the same quality of standard as a corporation. The same basic principles of providing support to executives, would work the same way in the church. The similarities have to do with, displaying professionalism, intelligence, competence, skills, abilities, respect, obedience, self-discipline, knowledge, and so much more. These characteristics are necessary and can work anywhere.

One of my most passionate and inspiring, God-given desires is to teach the temple/church office personnel strategies on how to be an effective and valued administrative professional. I endeavor to travel and share the strategies and methodologies I have learned and developed from the last 30 years of my professional career.

So, let's begin our journey together as we dive deep into the *Spine of the Temple*.

Spine of the Temple

When a person or family is considering settling down in a good church home, one of the many things they want to know is who is the pastor? What does he believe and teach? That's because the anointing that rests on the leader of the house should infiltrate the entire atmosphere of the church. The pastor's understanding, interpretation, illustration, and regurgitation of the Word of God is essential to the local church body. The word of God, when it is taught, preached or spoken, should have a mind-blowing impact. It has the amazing ability and power to change a life, save a soul, heal the sick, and raise the dead. The Word of God is quick and powerful, sharper than any double-edged sword (Hebrews 4:12). It is what attracts, engages, and sustains the sheep (members of the body of Christ). So then to settle in a church where the Word of God is going forth, in most cases for most people, you can thrive in the Spirit and in the natural.

To have *vision* means to have imagined the outcome before it's seen. It's the finished or completed picture of whatever has not yet manifested *(Lana's definition)*. The dictionary states that vision is: *something that is or has been seen; unusual competence in discernment of perception; intelligent foresight; the manner in which one sees or conceives of something; a mental image produced by the imagination.*

The pastor's vision given from God is what should be shared with the congregants and that vision motivates and activates the mission to be carried out by congregants, ministry leaders, church staff and others who are in support of the vision (Habakkuk

2:2). The pastor sees and hears directly from God and is shown a clear vision; the staff, leaders, and congregation are the ones who help bring the vision to life. The pastor is the leader who leads the entire body in the direction that the Lord has assigned for that group of congregants, who are also dwellers in the temple.

It's pretty clear that the pastor is extremely essential to the many aspects of the local church assembly, temple, and our ministry of congregants and groups. When this role's responsibilities are understood by all, you want to make efforts to do all that is necessary to preserve him or her. Sometimes how we preserve, assist, or care for the pastor will determine how the world will view them. Quality care of the priest/pastor/leader by the people he leads will help with having an effective and impactful leader.

Some leaders have very small or intimate size congregations and may only require minimal support provided by an admin, a finance team, and janitor for example. Other size congregations that exceed 100 congregants will practically have the same support staff, but their roles will be expanded vertically *(hierarchical)* and horizontally (teams, auxiliaries, units) to adequately support the existing structure. Adequate support for all size ministries is vital. No church or organization can be successful and efficient without administrative support. The overall administration would typically make certain that basic needs, wants, and ministry related desires are met so that the pastor can be given to prayer and other ministerial callings.

Much respect and consideration is given toward the role of the pastor/leader/executive because of the great assignment that has been ordained by our God. Constant reassurance and support for the pastor/leader is needed. If applicable, the first level of moral support should come from the spouse. This should result in the form of encouragement, love, and marital responsibilities being fulfilled emotionally, physically, mentally and possibly financially. Another level of support, which should work alongside the leader, is the administrative professional. This person coordinates, anticipates, engages, manages (subjective) the leader. There is usually one other person in this supportive role, who is necessary in the temple and that person's title can be any of the following: the pastor's administrator, executive assistant, administrative assistant, secretary, adjutant, armor-bearer, and so forth. Whatever the preferred title might be, this person is assigned to provide daily support to the pastor/leader.

Before I dive into the details of this important role, let me tell my story. Currently, I am in an executive administrator role within a mega-church. As said before, I've also held various administrative positions in different capacities within corporate America as well. All of my previous experiences, education, training, and personal development has afforded me the opportunity to write this book and tell you all about what I learned.

What I've learned is that no matter the industry you work in, when you are supporting a leader the expectations for your role as support person hardly differs. Serving senior leaders warrants a very strong, secure, mature, resilient, dependable, knowledgeable, and diligent person. That person is you and me, and we are executive assistants, executive admins, or secretaries. We have to be like rocks and glue all at the same time. The rock represents sustainability, endurance, resilience. The glue is exactly what you are thinking - it holds everything together, which is a very vital part of what we do. We hold things together to keep it from falling apart. We also cover, shield, and protect. Without either, we would be lopsided as assistants, and not operate in the most efficient manner.

Management is depending on us. As part of our role, we know the *who, what, when, where, why and how* of everything. Most often we are the liaisons between our leaders and the rest of the organization. We are usually the voice, the communicator, the messenger, the facilitator, the problem solver and so much more. The pastor/leader is the one who have the vision for the entire organization. They see the big picture of where the organization or living organism is going and it is their responsibility to convey the vision to the other leaders.

Habakkuk 2:2-3: *And the Lord answered me, and said, Write the vision, and make it plain upon tables, that he may run that readeth it. For the vision is yet for an appointed time, but at the end it shall speak, and not lie: though it tarry, wait for it; because it will surely come it will not tarry.*

The head of the church or organization needs all hands-on deck in support of the vision. The flow to accomplish the vision should funnel in the following order or something similar: vision, mission/goal, plan/strategy, execute, implementation. In most cases (possibly all) visions often touches all areas of the business or organization and will need to be supported by the teams identified in the plan/strategy. Knowing this, the project will at some point fall into the hands of the administrator to either type up, formulate a document or chart, etc.

Hence the title of the book, the spine as we know it is divided into five regions: cervical, thoracic, lumbar, sacrum and coccyx, and these five regions supports every part of the body. If there is any malfunctioning of any of the parts of the spine, the entire body is in trouble.

Administrative professionals are the spines. We have the responsibility to serve our leaders whether small or great. The heads, our leaders, gives us the vision, direction, and manual to follow. If we do not receive instruction from the leader, it becomes difficult to follow or know where we are going. Literally, without the spine and its components we wouldn't be able to walk, talk, or feel in some cases. It also impacts the control tower of our body, which is the brain. The spine is just that important. And so are we to our perspective organizations. Therefore, I wanted to share all the essential information I've learned, experienced, and discovered in the role of an executive assistant over the years in one easy-to-read book for you. I wanted to divulge all the secrets of my journey with everyone so we all can win. So please keep reading, take notes, and highlight whatever resonates with you. I pray that something in this book will help you be even greater at your assignment than you already are. Enjoy and God bless!

Chapter 1

The Most Important Role in the Church

Administrative/Executive Assistants are the backbones of any organization. They wear several hats at one time. If they are missing for a period of time normal operations are interrupted. It is equivalent to when mom is sick at home. The husband and kids can't figure out what to do.

Cervical - Neck anatomy is a well-engineered structure of bones, nerves, muscles, ligaments and tendons. The cervical spine (neck) is delicate - housing the spinal cord that sends messages from the brain to control all aspects of the body - while also remarkably strong and flexible, allowing movement in all

1

directions.

Let's Get This Day Started!

What does a day look like serving a high-level leader? Honestly, there is no simple way to answer this question. Every day is different. It brings about different experiences, challenges and responsibilities. Although the days are always different, some things must remain consistent, which is the person serving the leaders directly - the executive assistants, secretaries, or administrators.

Administrative professionals are the individuals who are responsible for the day-to-day operations that keep the leaders going from morning to night. We must be on task at all times. No matter the title the organization has given within this supportive role, the goal is that it should be widely understood that this person is the key to the effectiveness and success of the leader's daily activities. Leaders would not be as efficient and powerful in their roles because they would be attempting to handle things that an assistant is responsible for and lead at the same time. Without a good support staff, the leader would be functioning at a much lower capacity.

I have served pastors of all size congregations. If I displayed difficulty providing the daily expectations, the leaders wouldn't be able to arrive at the bedside of the sick. Perhaps they'd have difficulty organizing sermon notes, or would not make engagements or conferences, nor serve in excellence without me as the administrative support.

Some may not understand all that we handle for our leaders, but our position is heavy and loaded. How effective do you think a doctor would be without a nurse or a pilot without a flight attendant? The reality is that the sick wouldn't get healed and the flight won't take off without these significant people by their side. And a pastor, especially a high-profile pastor, couldn't soar as high without their assistant(s). There are several responsibilities that each one of us holds. It can vary from the industry and the size of the organizations. But some things remain the same and some things should be consistent across all levels. Efficient support is one of the key elements to this role.

Communication:

Being diligent about your professional communication is essential in any professional

4

environment, but in a church it's even more important. An admin to the pastor is considered information central. All things pertaining to the

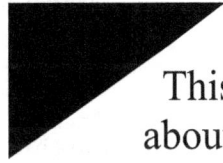

This is not about being nosy but being informed.

church comes through the key support staff. It is commonly said that if the key admin doesn't know about it, it doesn't exist or it's not happening. Admins are the closest people to a pastor outside of their spouse. So, this person should always know everything concerning the ministry and its operations. This is not about being nosy but being informed. In order to play the game, you must always know the instructions, rules, and those who are playing. This is the same for you in your various industries.

In order to get the mission accomplished, there

is much information that must be articulated through many channels to and from the admin. The admin is responsible for making the leader aware of his day, any scheduled meeting, conferences that have been booked, members who require visitation, prayer requests, staff needs, and so much more. There are many important issues and information in and outside the church that needs to be communicated to the pastor, especially if it directly affects the ministry.

Leaders also receive correspondence through mail, email, fax and telephone messages daily. It is imperative for accurate comprehension, timely responsiveness, and efficient prioritization, which is needed to make sure all items get addressed in a timely fashion and appropriately. In such cases as this, the admin will need to have excellent attention to detail, good judgement, and some analytical application to distribute the information accordingly. This goes beyond knowing how to type and send emails.

You must know how to respectfully address members of the clergy and executives from other organizations. Organize important documents, communicate well in conversations and be truthful, schedule appointments effectively all with the pastor's reputation in mind. Reason being is because you are his direct representative to the public. If you are unorganized, disrespectful, and unprofessional, everyone can, and will, assume that the pastor/leader behaves similarly. Admins are always operating on behalf of the pastor or leader of an organization. In understanding that concept, administrative responsibilities should be handled with the utmost respect and care. Always stay organized and professional with everything and everyone.

Operations

When working in any industry, things can change without notice depending on the needs of the house or business. Meetings move, appointments rescheduled, emergencies occur, and the leader may need to shift. Anything can happen at any time, making for an eventful situation for the admin.

Although it can become difficult at times when this happens, it is important for admins to always keep their cool and remain poised, calm, and professional. We must remain flexible and accommodating to everyone in order to get the situation handled. Whatever you do, *don't take anything personal* – especially if it's not directly effecting or causing an attack on your professional character. I can't stress this point enough - remember, in most cases it is not about you. There is often a conglomeration of things going on at one time that directly impacts the leader and may not include you at all. The best approach is to not think about yourself, but how you can better serve everyone involved in the organization. Unfortunately, admins will sometimes be inconvenienced, must work longer hours, and sometimes be challenged with not having the resources necessary to carry out an assignment. But a great tool to access is prayer. Consistently pray for swift creativity and innovativeness in order to appropriately handle any situation that arises. And remember no matter what happens, always stay in a positive, accommodating, and respectful temperament.

Event Planning

There are various operations that admins must coordinate for leaders. One of the most challenging can be event planning. This could be a corporate event, anniversary, birthday celebration, or even a large ministry conference. No matter what the occasion, admins are the event specialists. I don't say this just because of our creativity or understanding of details, but because we know what our leaders want. All details matter, but the most important ones are what are specific to your leader. Their vision, desires, and expected outcomes for any event have to always be considered when planning begins. Admins are key players in this process because they know the leader's voice and heart. They must be involved in the entire process to make sure every coordinator involved understands that concept. They must maintain the position as the sounding voice in the room that always puts their leader's vision before that of a personal desire for an event. So be ready! This can be a planned expectation or something that suddenly arises as a need.

Chapter 2

The Right and Left Hand

(The Primary Resource)

In order to fully support your leader and provide the best service possible, you must first know them and their expectations.

Head of House

No matter the title of who you serve, you must know who they are before you can become successful at your job. Whether you are in ministry, business, healthcare, or education understanding who you serve is the main key to being a great support person.

So, what should you know about them? Just

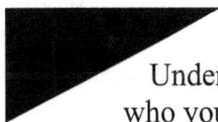

Understanding who you serve is the main key to being a great support person. about everything. You have to understand the role that they are in and what comes with it. You must know their likes and dislikes. What makes them happy and what makes them angry? You have to know what their needs are daily and be very concerned about meeting them.

Happy Leaders

Serving any leader comes with some highs and some lows. Challenges arise daily, sometimes a few times a day. But an effective administrator tries their best to get ahead of that. And truly knowing and understanding your leader can help you do just that. The first thing is to provide what they need and want sometimes even before they ask for it. This would involve you taking the initiative at times. To be upfront, not all leaders are comfortable with you jumping ahead of them and making things happen without their knowledge. They may fear that you could possibly know too much and reconsider your position. But most leaders would love to not have to guide you through every single step of serving them. Most executives will appreciate you thinking outside the box and being creative about solutions before they even know it's a problem. Being innovative could place your leader in a better position, make their days lighter, and ultimately make them happy. And a happy boss means a happy support team! The goal is to have things work out for everyone. But again, you must know your leader and what tasks they are and are not comfortable with you handling.

If you are uncertain to what you should or should not do for your leader, always ask them. Just asking them about their level

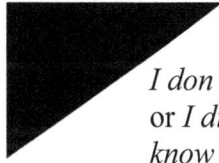

I don't know or *I didn't know* should not be words you use when conferring with your boss.

of comfortability and expectations from you is a great way to ensure that everyone is on the same page. I would rather you ask than not ask. The worst thing you can do as an administrator is assume or don't know. Try not to use the phrases, *I don't know,* or *I didn't know*. This will only frustrate your leader, the better way of avoiding saying these terms is to always ask questions. *I don't know* or *I didn't know* should not be words you use when conferring with your boss. No one expects you to be perfect or a mind reader. So, when in doubt, do what you can to find out the answer.

Heartbeat

We hear in ministry all the time that we need to have the heartbeat of the leader. What does that mean? Although there are many interpretations, it simply means to be on the same page with your leader. Having your leader's heartbeat is good to have because it means you understand what their vision and mission is for the organization. Having their heartbeat gives you a clear understanding of their desires. It helps you know the whole person you are serving. What kind of person they are and their behaviors. This is not something that will happen immediately. This is a progressive connection you will develop after time of working closely with them.

As previously stated, understanding the mission of the organization is part of developing the heartbeat of your leader. You begin to understand what they want, why they exist, where they want to go, and ultimately achieve. No matter the organization, understanding the purpose of the organization helps align the daily goals and tasks with the organization's mission. It provides a reason for why you are doing what you do. Even from something small as opening an email to building out an event. The *why* motivates your *how*.

Expectancy

Taking time to learn the specifics of the assignment or job can help guide you through the expectancy of your responsibilities. Most of your basic level of responsibilities are displayed in the job description. But most of your learned responsibilities will come as you grow within the organization, and your leader begins to trust who you are and what you are capable of doing. In your interview, the questions may have been very task specific to find out what you could, would, or should do in certain situations. But it's not until you're operating in that task that you're really going to know what you are capable of. No matter what the expectation is, make habit out of attempting to exceed expectations. This is so, very gratifying for the leader – and ultimately puts you in a high-level of respect amongst your leader. If the leader only expects level two from you, attempt to perform at a level five. This just simply means always go over and beyond expectations to achieve success in every task assigned. As you do more than expected, more tasks will be given to you. Don't look at the added workload as more work, but look at it as you're gaining more insight, knowledge, wisdom, and experience within your organization. And this also indicates that your leader trusts you... isn't that great? You never know what doors will open for you when you're operating in *excellence.*

Let me provide you a personal example. When I was first hired for my most recent position, I came in as a part-timer to be responsible for managing an executive's calendar and schedule and was the assistant to his executive admin or his administrator. Now this was very different for me because I have had a ton of experience working in corporate America as an executive administrator supporting C-Suite executives. I have experience in supporting investors and bankers in the financial field. I've also worked for Oprah Radio, the Chairman of Johnson Publishing Company, the CEO of JPC, the CFO of Mesirow,

Accenture Consulting, the President of Merrill Lynch Business Financial Services Division, and more. I've been placed in positions where I've met many famous entertainers and celebrities just by coming to work every day. I've always worked closely with senior

> A job is what you do for a check. But your assignment is what you are called and chosen to do so that your life's purpose can be fulfilled.

management and C-Suite executives. Therefore, to enter an organization with a salary of only a fraction of what I was accustom to and supporting someone who I had relatively equal skillset to was a bit of a challenge. But I had to do it because it was my divine assignment at the time. I learned that a job is what you do for a check. But your assignment is what you are

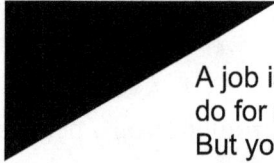

called and chosen to do so that your life's purpose can be fulfilled.

However, in this part-time role, I exceeded far beyond the expectations. I'm sure the organization leaders thought they were getting someone who would just do basic clerical work, but I was capable of doing the work of a strategic manager. I expected that when someone noticed my level of experience, the position I would be offered would complement my decorated background. I then noticed that God was up to something. I was experiencing a change and shift in my life.

Sometime before I applied for my current role, I was laid off from a job where I was making a substantial amount of money, my salary was sweet! When I was suddenly laid off, it was very devastating to me. I realized that eighty percent of my income was gone, which lead me on my quest to find additional income quickly. After a long search, I was finally able to land a job. However, the job I accepted only paid me a little over the minimum wage. Now understand this, a year prior I was in a position making six figures to suddenly eating some delicious humble pie with my next position. Although I trusted God and knew He was up to something, this was very devastating for me, but I was obedient. Because I had been seeking a new position for so long, I accepted the part-time role because I knew I had to start somewhere.

I started as a part-time assistant. I was responsible for managing the executive calendar and coordinating his travel arrangements. Initially, there weren't too many expectations of me, I just needed to handle the specific tasks given and complete my daily assignments. But of course, I went in performing beyond the expectations that were set before me. I began by finding ways to do my simple tasks more effectively and efficiently. I started to create forms, documents, make professional recommendations based on my previous decade-long corporate experience and developing more expert-level practices. I wanted to ensure that the leader I was serving had everything he deserved at an executive level. I did not let my title or pay determine the level of excellence I brought to my role. I put in the same effort as if I was still making that six-figure income. My integrity and level of respect in my assignment remained the same, and eventually it was noticed.

Before I knew it, an opportunity came to me for a full-time executive administrator position directly serving the senior pastor. Guess what? I took it! My acceleration to this new level was a reward for my commitment to excellence. The root word for excellence is excel – if you're not actively performing in excellence you should start on your very next day at work. I was recognized for the value I brought to my previous role, despite the expectations that were placed upon me. In my eyes, I wasn't doing anything special. I am a person of integrity and honesty, and I always make a conscious effort to operate in the spirit of excellence regardless of the opportunity.

Unbeknownst to me, others in the office were having conversations about my work performance and my reputation was making its way up to the people who had the power to change my position. These particulars were shared with the CEO and as a result a recommendation was made for me to receive the executive level full-time position.

This position was such a blessing. I've been

blessed to not only utilize the skills and expertise I had already possessed, but at the same time I've learned a few other things of grandeur which has taken me higher than before. I know that I would have missed this great opportunity if I did not operate at a higher level of expectancy from the beginning. This is why I encourage you to do the same.

Chapter 3

It's Not What You Say But How You Say It

Administrative positions are typically the initial point of contact for staff and members. The delivery of service rather physical or verbal is extremely important. You are a direct representation of your leader and/or church.

We have all learned how important good communication is to any business, organization, or person. It's not all about what you say, but also the tone by which you use and your intentions when you say it. This is special for me because I once was in a unique situation within the organization where I work. I functioned in two different roles directly relating to the CEO of the organization.

Effective communication is premier in any profession, especially when you are in a support staff position. Again, you are the liaison essentially between the executive or leader and their various departments, vendors, and other professional contacts. Having the ability to articulate needs, requests, wants, and expectations to a second, third, or group party is crucial to your role.

While essential, it's not just about understanding the written form of communication such as subject verb agreement, proper nouns, verbs, adverbs adjectives, propositional phrases, etc. Your posture, tones, appearance and presence also play an important role in how you communicate and are

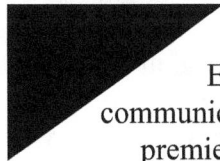

> Effective communication is premier in any profession, especially when you are in a support staff position.

perceived by others. Having the ability to say words with true meaning and in the proper context.

Speaking proper English confidently is a good sign of a polished individual. If this isn't a strong quality for you, I would suggest some online courses, or even YouTube, to brush up on skills. There are numerous tutorials available on YouTube, free of charge. This is important because you want to be able to convey messages and speak intelligently and be understood wherever you go. You want others to be able to grasp what you need so that you can become effective in what you are doing. Your ability to be successful in certain tasks weighs heavily on how you understand and the way you express yourself. This is very important, right? You want to be heard and understood. You may also want the message you convey to evoke action. I'm not trying to make you feel bad or inadequate, I just know the negative and positive impact of effective communication. The impact of it all is instant and the goal of our communication is for it to come off as positive.

Verbal communication is great, but don't neglect the impact of non-verbal communication either. BUSINESSDICTIONARY.COM puts it this way: verbal communication is the sharing of information between individuals by using speech and communication that employs readily understood spoken words, as well as ensuring that the enunciation, stress, and tone of voice with the words expressed is appropriate. Non-verbal communication is the transmission of messages or signals through a non-verbal platform, such as eye contact, facial expressions, gestures, posture, and the distance between two individuals (Wikipedia).

Non-verbal communication speaks volumes without saying a word. This is the visible communication that everyone sees before you even say hello. It starts with how you are dressed, your facial expressions, your posture, and the position of your hands, your complete physical presentation and gestures. You can scream without speaking with how you carry yourself. How you present yourself physically, depending on the audience that you're speaking to can determine whether you'll be accepted or rejected. Depending on the environment, you may want to mimic what is acceptable and safe. You want to be able to carry yourself from various environments while always remaining professional and respectful. Always keep in mind that your customers in any environment are important. Your customers are who you communicate with daily. No matter if you are working in the White House or the barbershop, your look should represent the brand you serve under. And you always want to represent your brand well.

Again, no matter the environment at any given time, as mentioned in the previous chapter, you should always remain truthful and honest when communicating with anyone. This means to never communicate on things you don't know and be mindful of communicating things you do know. It's not always wise to tell everything you know. Always play it safe with conversations you can intelligently speak to. A major rule of thumb is less is more and safe. Don't embarrass yourself by having conversations based on assumptions or things you know are not true. Almost immediately, it will take away your credibility. If you find yourself in a situation like this, always inquire about obtaining more information for points of understanding.

I don't always agree with following after your assumptions (taking too much for granted; presumptuous) because it could come back to bite you later and cause some professional damage to you and your career. So, the best advice I could give you is to be yourself. Always remain comfortable. Ask questions when unclear on anything. I would rather you be inquisitive than develop false responses appearing to be the truth. Take a subtle approach to new things. Don't dominate an area that is new. Stay teachable and confident in posture, and always be willing to learn more in all environments.

Written Communication

We live in a predominately digital world. Everything is online, in email, and so forth. Written communication is almost fifty percent or more of what you do. The days of mailing letters through the United States Post Office are almost extinct. Your communication is recorded instantly and downloadable for others to share immediately. Needless to say, your written communication needs to be spectacular. Your written correspondence may be at the desks of senior management, chief executive officers, dignitaries, pastors, and all other high-level offices. And some of your work could also be entertained by the everyday person who is reading up on you or your organization. Whatever and whomever the person, they are expecting for communication to be accurate, relevant, and understandable.

Professional communication should not be written in shorthand or text message versions. The body of written work should be in complete formatting using all proper verbiage. You always want readers to be able to interpret exactly the message you are conveying. If at all possible, always try to eliminate any room for confusion or doubt. Sometimes we are not the best writers, but we know people who are, allow them to review your work or inquire about your work with someone, just to be sure.

Always address the proper order of hierarchy when sending any form of professional communication. The hierarchy order leaders should be listed in an email is: COO, vice president, senior manager, managers, etc. This is also appropriate when cc'ing, memos, organizational charts, and so forth. This is important to show respect for the chain of command in all areas. Some organizations are stricter on this than others, but to ensure you are always covered, always follow the chain of command. When you address everyone in order, the next step is to monitor your written tone.

Please stay away from saying anything negative or unprofessional in an email. For one, it's not professional, and for two, once your words are out there in cyberspace, you cannot get them back. So, if you do not feel comfortable saying something in person to someone as an effort to prevent confrontation, it is safe to say that you should not say it in an email either. Always make your emails friendly and warm. Greetings and salutations are always a plus. Keep your language clear and concise. Don't use harmful words or engage in a virtual debate via email. If things begin to get unfriendly, always suggest that further communication be made offline in a face-to-face meeting.

Meeting Decorum

When preparing for a meeting, always know the agenda, have items ready to discuss, and as a nice relationship building tool, give participants a heads up that their names are on the agenda. This gives them a chance to present with efficiency, moves the meeting along faster, and prevents the leader from being upset when questions can't be answered. Depending on the type of meeting, make sure you have what's needed for everyone to be successful. For instance, a projector, television screen, virtual conference calling, dry erases boards, and anything else that contributors may need to convey their portion of the meeting. You want to always be ready and make sure that all involved in a meeting is prepared as well. Have things arranged and set up beforehand, especially technology. It's always a good idea to test technology prior to meetings or conferences. You want your meetings and conferences to always go well; strive for no hiccups. Some things you may not be able to prevent, so always have a back-up plan such as printed materials on hand just in case.

Effective Note Taking

Now this is not one of my favorite skills, but it is very important in meetings. This is crucial because the main points of the meeting, follow-up items, and new assignments must always be recorded. I know how to take my own notes but taking well-detailed notes to be entered into a shared portal or database I can do it; however, I prefer not. And I own that and have no problem expressing it. So, to make sure this is something that can still be covered, I abase myself and allow others to handle this assignment. I have a co-worker who is extremely effective at note taking and has the skillset to perform this duty with tremendous expertise. She types so fast that she could be a court reporter. But because I recognized my weakness, I was able to lean on someone for their strength, this task is successfully handled regularly. You may or may not have someone to assist you with this. And if you don't, always consider audio recording the meetings and having them transcribed later as a resource. Keep in mind for audio recorded meetings, you must have written permission from everyone to record the meetings.

When taking notes, please make sure you are listening carefully. You don't have to capture every word or idea verbatim, but you do need to understand the concept of the idea, a resolution to a problem, the person speaking, and any additional key components to the meeting. Recording specific timelines as well is a great item to make sure you note as well. Due dates of expectations and assignments must be recorded because they are essential to continued business. Try not to attempt to fill in blanks that you may have missed. You don't want to fabricate any information in written notes.

Written Letters

Although most of your correspondence for your leader will be via email, some letter writing may be needed. If so, the same concept goes for emails but with a more formal and traditional approach. The usage of proper grammar, addressing the correct person, date and greeting/salutation messages are all necessary. When writing a letter, there is a specific format that must be followed as well. *Please research proper letter writing essentials and formats to view professional letter example.*

Letter writing should always be on professional letterhead when coming from the desk of your leader. Ensure that contact information for the recipient is correct as well so that important information is presented to the right person. Try to always make letters precise and exact to prevent messages from being too long. Close each letter with a signature along with contact information from the sender in the event that there are additional questions for you to answer.

Make sure letters are clean and free of finger marks when being placed in envelopes. Presentation is everything, so you don't want others to open your letter and know what you had for lunch. So always handle letters with care and clean hands.

Greeting Guests

Treat all your guests the same. No matter if they come in with a suit jacket or with no shoes. Always show respect and express consideration for them and their individual needs. Your response should always be appropriate and welcoming. As one of my coworkers says, "Make people feel warm and fuzzy!' That just simply means make everyone who comes through your doors feel at home. Don't change your posture, language, or consideration based on what they look like. Always remain the same. The guest is simply that - a guest. And that guest deserves great respect and treatment at all times.

Everybody should be greeted with a smile, a handshake, and then offered a seat, water and/or coffee. Once they are all settled and have informed you of the purpose of their visit (in most cases you may already know why and who they're coming to visit), offer to help them with their belongings, and if needed, escort them to their destination. Give them an opportunity to ask questions and always try to provide an answer for them so they feel that their time with you was worth the visit. Always remember to take care of your guests as if they were one of your family members. You are more than likely going to be the primary face of the organization for most people. Make your first impression a good one to remember.

Chapter 4

Work Smart Not Hard

Knowledge is power. What is done with that knowledge is key to your success. A number of daily responsibilities and expectations of someone in the role of administrative support staff is the use of technology. If you know what systems to use for what you need to get done, you will operate more effectively in time and management.

Knowledge is power is like a model or just something that I choose to live by. There is always a better way, or a more efficient way to do something. I often try to avoid complexity. If something appears to be hard or difficult, I am sure to take a moment and

43

find out if there is a better way to do it. It usually comes to mind that there must be a less complicated way of figuring this out. I choose to work smarter not harder. A couple things I ponder when trying to simplify - effectiveness and efficiency. Is there a different way to do it and get either the same outcome or better outcome, and/or how much time will it take? Can I do more in less time with the strategy that I'm currently working with? I do this even if it means that I have to let go and delegate a specific task to someone who can do it better than me. Working smarter also means understanding that there is someone that is better than me in areas I struggle in. I don't waste time trying to fumble with tasks I can't do when there is someone who has already mastered it. The smartest way to work is to know your weaknesses and don't be too proud to ask for help. You can't do it all. You should have the knowledge and resources available to you so that you can access it at any time - even if it means you have to resend it, or phone a friend – it's absolutely worth it.

When you empower yourself, you understand it, you know it, share it, and you use it when necessary. This is based on your knowledge, your interpretation, and your awareness of everything. Tech tools, computer software programs, apps, and social media are all essential to your empowerment as well. When you have the knowledge, you become a vital participant in daily responsibilities and decisions. However, on the contrary, knowledge can also work against you. This is because sometimes what you know can cause you to hold back or become reluctant to be a part of a specific task. It can cause procrastination or a situation of you not moving

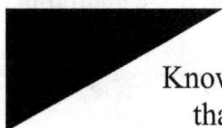

> Knowledge is that special power that no one can take away from you.

forward because of fear. Fear can prevent you from taking risks that could be a breakthrough to and for your success. Although knowledge is very powerful, it can be a weakness if you allow it to. This can occur when you are not comfortable or confident in yourself. I encourage you to build that confidence and take those risks which can ultimately bring about the greatest results in your career.

Although risks do not always guarantee one hundred percent positive outcomes all the time, sometimes it's just worth the effort. Effort is the use of physical or mental energy to do something; a difficult exertion of strength. Knowledge is that special power that no one can take away from you. Knowledge is the state or fact of knowing; familiarity; awareness or understanding through experience or study (dictionary.com). The knowledge, your knowledge, that you've acquired from school, experiences, relationships, and observations is specific to you. No one else has it like you, and no one else can utilize it the way you can. It's yours and cannot be confiscated. Learn to use what's inside of you and allow it to be displayed on the outside so that the world can see it. You decide when to take it out and lay it on the table. You can put it in your pocket and hold it back if you want. Regardless of how you use it, the most important thing is that you are using it. It's a valuable tool to have. Use it to empower yourself and bring forth confidence because you are the expert in what you know. Treat it as such and never forget it. It's yours exclusively.

Here is something to think about, knowledge is not always what you've learned in school. Everyone doesn't attend college, nor does everyone have a degree. You can gain knowledge in various ways to help you throughout your career and life in general. You can do your own research by reading books, taking online courses, visiting YouTube, having a conversation with someone, listening to the radio or podcast, and more. However, you obtain it, understand that you worked to get it. And whatever you decide to do with it is up to you.

It is most important to always be willing to continuously receive more knowledge so that you never stop learning your craft. Sharpen your skills often. This is especially true after you have accomplished something great. Never get too comfortable because you have now set a bar that you must keep climbing. Stay sharp and always look for ways to improve.

Technology

Again, as leaders in any field, we must recognize that there is always someone better than the next in all areas. Someone else has done things differently and in a better way. Someone has developed a system or created a shortcut to a program that will make life easier for everyone. People are creating new things every day. The one thing that changes almost daily is technology. Understanding and using technology to its advantage will surely make your daily tasks more

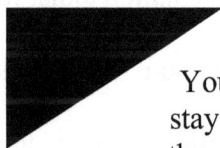

You want to stay ahead of the game and become savvy with technology systems before there is a need.

successful. Having knowledge about various computer software, apps, and programs can help you navigate and troubleshoot through the various problematic office situations with ease. You don't have to be a technology expert but familiarizing yourself with the basics of some programs is a must.

Some of the tools to know would be the systems used for phone and video conferences, Microsoft Word, presentation tools, webinars systems, and more. Depending on the leader you serve and the environment you are in, technology can control literally everything that you do.

I work for a leader that is internationally known. He is always traveling across the world preaching and training people. With his lifestyle, my daily tasks can be extremely demanding. Technology is essential for me because having to book travel accommodations, communicate or convey needs, coordinate schedules, manage calendars, and prepare itineraries. This regularly involves me speaking over the phone a lot, but also using video conference systems, tracking systems, computer programs, and much more. It's never a down or slow moment. I have to get meetings and appointments started in a timely fashion. Being comfortable with technology and all of its benefits helps me become better at what I do. I understand that technology may be scary to some people, but I encourage you to learn as much as you can. And don't try to learn it as you go. You want to stay ahead of the game and become savvy with technology systems before there is a need. You don't want to stumble and figure things out while you are on the spot. That can be embarrassing and make you look less professional. Take the time and invest in yourself by learning all you can by using the tools that are available to you.

Realize that we need technology more now than we ever have. In today's time, we can't live without it. Not knowing how to operate a computer can be detrimental. Make an attempt to understand what you don't know by staying engaged with the activities happening around you. Read and watch the news and other informational mediums to learn about what is going on.

Social media is another platform by which you can stay engaged and learn more about what's new and exciting. You'll also be introduced to the latest and greatest trends, and other on-topic things that may need to be discussed. Don't stress about not being a master at it. Learn enough so that you can intelligently navigate through the platforms and systems. Once you have the basic understanding of something, push yourself to transition to an intermediate and advanced phase of any component of it.

You can advance your in-depth knowledge by learning a little bit more from personal research, online classes, and studying under someone who is already an expert. It's always good to communicate with others in your field to see what's going on out there and what everybody is doing just to keep yourself up-to-par with relevant information. It will always benefit you to stay one step in front of yourself in all areas so you will never fall behind.

Chapter 5

Presentation is Everything

It is human nature for people to eat with their eyes first. This means that if it looks good, it must be good for you. That's what people think when they meet you. If you look the part, the assumption is you'll be able to handle the position.

Look the Part

First impressions are the most lasting impressions. What people see is what they feel they are going to get. Taking pride and ownership in the entire package that is of yourself. What you're presenting is crucial. What you wear, how you smell, the way you walk, what you do, what you say and how you say it, your confidence and attitude are all part of the total you. I can't express enough how important your overall initial self-presentation is for setting the tone for a positive and engaging outcome. You determine how others will perceive you by how you present yourself to others.

First impressions are the most lasting impressions.

I have over thirty years of working in corporate America. During those years, no matter what professional industry I worked in, I understood that my appearance at work each day was very important. Your appearance can determine the level of respect you will receive from others. Yes, you can gain a lot of respect because of how you look and vice versa, you can get little to no respect looking any kind of way. I've worked in media and entertainment, financial firms, consulting industry, communications, airlines, securities firms, governmental agencies and more, with the expectations that I needed to come to work daily dressed respectably. Although today, some environments are more relaxed and dress codes have become more lenient, your personal representation should always shout professional even when you're dressed casually. You only get one chance for a person to observe you and determine your capabilities, character, and value of work. So, if you want the first impression to be a good one, always allow your attire to be at its best.

While growing in my professional experiences, I was always taught to wear a suit jacket. The suit jacket was a sign of authority and leadership in many environments. Have you ever noticed your behavior toward a person with a suit jacket? Majority of professionals wear conservative clothing or business casual attire. This excludes jeans, gym-shoes, t-shirts, and other items that can be seen at a baseball game or at a concert. In corporate, women are expected to wear considerably the same style however with an emphasis on hair, makeup, and accessories. Although hairstyles today are more expressive of a person's personality, very modest and tamed styles are expected. Makeup is very clean and not loud, along with perfume and earrings. The phrase *less is more* is typically used in more professional settings. The point here is, if you want to play safe, keep it very mild and modern. Stay clear of extreme distracting garments. Avoid anything that will bring attention to yourself in a negative way.

What I stated above is the traditional expectations for professional attire. In the contemporary environment, a lot has changed tremendously. Although the traditional approach is more comfortable and safer, in a contemporary environment you will find a lot more leniency with attire than in a traditional setting. The modern, contemporary environments permit the more casual and laid-back attire. No jacket or specific special dress are expected. Many environments allow jeans and polo shirts. It's all up to the organization and the culture that was created. Although my recommendation is to always do a little better than expected, know where you are and do what makes you comfortable while staying in compliance. Complying is the more important concept to whatever attire you wear. When you are in compliance, you feel confident, which ultimately leads you to being more effective in whatever task you are conquering. Overall, try to understand and learn the culture of your work environment. Add your personal style to what's expected and be the best you at all times.

Today, styles are changing all the time. New trends are set every day just about. These trends can alter what's expected in hair styles and clothing looks for men and women. Different trends are accepted in different professional settings. Some trendy fashions are too harsh for the work environments, but some are excitingly acceptable. One trend that is very new but great to see is natural hair styles for African American women. Traditionally all hair styles were expected to mimic a European culture. But now, more African American women are expressing their cultural diversity by wearing their natural hair. These styles vary from afros, French braids, curly up-dos, and more. Dreadlocks are even becoming more popular today than ever before. And being an African American woman, I think it's great. And I hope that other cultures can feel comfortable exhibiting their natural selves in a professional manner at work.

Now that we have a good idea of what we should and should not wear, let's not forget how important self-grooming is as well. Grooming is having a consistent handle on your personal maintenance. Getting a regular haircut, keeping facial appearances clean and clear, wearing an appropriate amount of cologne and keeping well-manicured nails are all just as important as your clothes. One great example is for men who work in financial environments. This industry prefers a very clean-cut look for men. They prefer you to steer away from facial hair, beards, and mustaches. They prefer that all men keep their faces always easily recognizable, yet consistent. Now if you are working in education, your facial hair isn't an issue. It all depends on where you work and what the professional climate is requiring. Do your research because you don't want to work in a place that may require you to change something on yourself that you love. Nothing is worth altering who you are as a person. It never hurts to ask questions on all things before you accept a position anywhere.

Although it should not have to be said, but maintaining good hygiene is a must when working in any professional environment. Your professional image can be altered if you carry an odor with you daily. Remember to shower and use appropriate hygiene products. No one wants to work in an office space with someone that doesn't care about their personal hygiene. This is especially true for people in our roles. We meet and greet so many people for our leaders, that a bad aroma could impact the success of a meeting or conference. So, to be on the safe side always practice great cleanliness. If not for yourself than for everyone else that you work with. And besides, being clean and fresh provides you with great confidence. And confidence is great for you completing an assignment successfully, because when you feel good, you do good.

Appropriate Language

Using appropriate language in the workplace as an executive assistant is very important. Remember, we are information central for the entire organization. What we say and how we say it is paid close attention to. It's recorded and held at a high standard. It's also referenced in various meetings, conversations, and emails. This makes it essential that the way we speak and what we say exactly must be, not only accurate, but appropriate as well. Our grammar should be used correctly. We should refrain from

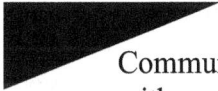

> Communicating with respect for them and yourself.

using offensive language, slang, and profane terms. This should not be done in verbal or written communication. We must be able to speak to whatever audience effectively, so it's important to know who exactly our audience is. We have to keep in mind that we are the speaker that others are listening to for confirmation of something, direction or permission. Whomever your audience, be able to speak to the level they understand without being offensive and condescending; communicating with respect for them and yourself.

Professional Office Space

Depending on where your office space is and what your responsibilities are can determine how your environment should look. Either you are in a space where you are the first face customers see when they come into the building or you are behind the scenes making things happen and don't see anyone besides your leader. Those two scenarios have different presentation expectation but both in general should be clean and functional.

Let me give you an example. I don't greet anyone that comes through our organization's doors, this is what the receptionist does. I am on the executive floor on the upper level surrounded by the CEO, COO, and executive business manager. A great deal of my interactions is with people over the phone and the other happens outside of my office. I don't really have traffic in my office, so my office is most often always consumed with time-oriented assignments. I have large post-it notes on my wall because I brainstorm a lot. And in my brainstorming, so many ideas come so quickly that I need to get them out right away. Having them on the large note paper allows me to frequently look at them so it can trigger something else that may be required the next day that I may need to handle immediately. It's kind of like my running a tab of ideas, tasks, and thoughts that I need to address.

One of my coworkers told me that my office looks like a situation room. He named it that because there is so much going on in there that it looks like situations happen daily. And I love it and totally agree. It's organized chaos that I understand and that helps me be efficient at what I do. In this situation room, I'm thinking and visually making these thoughts come to life. I get to see what I'm thinking and review it at all at once. I know what's hanging up in my office and why. It may not appear to be as clean to the average person's office or desk, but I assure you it's clean. It's just organically organized to my preference. There is no food in my office or mishandling of items. It isn't cluttered or junky, it's just filled with things that I need on a more regular basis. And remember I don't have people or clients in my office. If for some reason I need to conduct a meeting or have some paperwork reviewed for my leader, I book a conference room. I never use my office. That's my workstation and I don't want outsiders to think that I am not professional because they don't understand my personal chaos.

If your office is in an open space like a welcome center or lobby, your workstation must remain clean at all times. You and your space are the first impression of the organization. If your station is filthy, unorganized and unpresentable, the assumption is going to be that organization is the same way. Stay away from eating food at your desk. Try to take your lunch away from your workstation so it doesn't smell or have debris from it either. Organize your station so that things are easy to find such as phone extensions, pamphlets, folders, etc. This gives a visitor an impression that you are well put together and prepared for whatever they may need - this is always a plus. With presentation being everything, you have to always be well put together, even at your workstation.

Your station should not be a place where everyone gathers to hang out either. The entrance should always remain peaceful with a subtle noise, nothing too loud. It should have a pleasant or neutral aroma. And the welcome should always be warm.

Meeting Spaces

No matter where your workstation or office is, oftentimes those in our role have to conduct or prep spaces for meetings. Organizing a conference area is a must. Your tasks for a meeting can go from creating the agenda, preparing presentation materials, setting up audio/visual technology, and preparing refreshments for all of the participants. If the task is big or small, always handle it with excellence. You want to make sure that you know who the audience is and what their needs would be. This is another way of staying ahead of the game. Knowing who you are prepping for can give you an idea of what things they may have forgotten about, and an opportunity for you to have it there already. That goes back to working smart and not hard. The more prepared you are, the more impressed your leader and others will be with your innovative and swift follow ups. Ensure that the area is clean before and after each meeting. Several people utilize conference areas, so it is a revolving door. You always want to make sure another meeting isn't delayed because you left things behind. Take ownership of making sure that all things are returned and stationed the way it was originally.

Professional Presentation Materials

Now that you have the conference space all set up, something else you want to make sure you have perfected are the materials. Oftentimes your leader may want you to create a presentation for them. If this happens, don't panic. It's actually a really good sign that your leader trusts you so much that they are relying on you to guide them through a specific meeting. You will be fine. All you need to know is who the audience is, what the topics are, where your notes are, and what resources are needed. You must know if the leader wants to read off a paper or cue card, or if they want to actually have a formal visual presentation. This would be a great time to know how to use the various Microsoft or Apple presentation programs. Some of them are PowerPoint, Presi, Canva, and Keynote for example. If you don't know any of these, it's time to learn. Not knowing is not even an excuse when there are online classes and even free tutorials that will assist anyone with learning anything new. This includes how to master using presentation software.

You don't want to not have this skillset. Presentations are inevitable. They happen all the time in professional settings. Especially when you serve a senior executive, pastor or high-level leader. And if you want to be the best support team member, you have to be able to provide assistance in any circumstance. A professional meeting or conference is a setting you want to excel in. Other executives and possible outside entities will be observing your professionalism and how well you handle yourself. You never know who will be around and what opportunity it may present. You have to always stay ready. And the only way to stay ready is to be ready. Be ready to set up, create, navigate, assist, breakdown and more. Sharpen your skills in all areas, especially technology. Sometimes it's all on you to get things right. Go into a meeting early to set up, prepare the space and test the

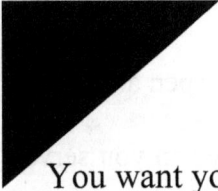

You want your meetings and conferences to always go well, strive for no hiccups.

programs needed. This will help you fix a potential problem before the general body enters the meeting. Always stay prepared. Always be ready.

Chapter 6

First Things First

There are so many tasks that lands in this role daily. Some routine and some spontaneous. The best way to tackle each thing effectively is to know how to prioritize according to importance.

Precedence Over Preference

There is no better feeling than knowing that you have completed all your tasks. Particularly those that are most important. Completed tasks from the most important to the least, makes you feel like you have conquered something. There are a great number of tasks that are assigned to you on a daily basis and it is imperative for your personal gratification to master knocking out the routine items first. This can make your day go a lot smoother.

Some routine items would be something like checking your emails, checking your voicemails, and if you're like me you'll have a task list that is prepared the day before that needs to be taken care of first thing the next morning. For instance, if there's some things that I didn't get completed on the day before, then I'll write them down to carry over for the next day. I try to take care of these items right away before assignments for the current day begin to pile up.

Depending on what your responsibilities are, some other tasks to do first thing in the morning could pertain to the office itself. For example, I'm responsible for setting the atmosphere physically. I make everyone feel comfortable in their perspective spaces. I turn the lights on, set the appropriate temperature, place the fragrances or oils on and sometimes I even straighten up the kitchen area in the event someone stays after me and forgets to put things back. I'm the one everyone comes to for a little burst of energy midway through the day, so I make sure the office candy jars are filled with a mixture of candy to make everyone happy.

This excites the employees and some of our office guests. I know what my leader likes to eat or snack on throughout the day, so I make sure the office refrigerator is stocked with those items for their comfort.

Although these tasks are not something that is laid out in my job description, I know what needs to be done and just take care of it. It makes the office more comfortable for everyone and sets us apart from others. Some additional tasks are to communicate with the cleaning crew to make sure all trash is taken out and bathrooms are clean. This is especially important for my leader's office space and the multipurpose conference rooms. These spaces are of high priority and must be adequately set up for meetings, planned and unplanned. Which then takes me to printing off the calendars, so my leader knows what to expect for the day. I place them on his desks for easy access.

Checking inventory of items needed in the office from stationary to printing paper is always a must. There are so many tasks that you can set as routine that should be taken care of at the beginning of the day. It all depends on where you are and what the needs would be. But getting these expected items out of the way can make it easier for you to handle the things coming up that can't be planned for or that are definitely more pressing.

These things discussed previously are what I do to set the atmosphere for the work environment I am currently in. It is just for comfort and appearances. But the business task list is a little different. The first thing you want to always do is check voicemails and emails. Typically, those are very important and need to be prioritized as such. I would have to say emails and voicemails would take precedence over everything unless there is an emergency of some sort that arises. Going through voicemails and emails can take some time. You want to make sure you respond appropriately and timely to your audience. These are items that are time stamped and trackable. So, try not to have someone wait more than 24-48 hours for a response. That's an easy way to have a complaint made against you. Stay on top of those assignments.

Besides, depending on what happens throughout the day, items in those messages could provide you an important assignment that deserves your attention. Emails alone can give you enough to handle for the entire day depending on what information it contains and who it is from.

Prioritizing

Prioritizing the rest of your day is major. You want to select what's the most important to the least. Although everything you do is important, some items take precedence over others. I can't necessarily tell you what those items would be because it all depends on your industry and leader. But know that anything that has a time stamped deadline must be completed on time. And on time should be considered to be early.

Try your best to never complete any assignment late. It doesn't look professional and gives the impression that you didn't care about how that item affected your organization. Your goal should always be to turn items around in a timely and a prompt manner even if there isn't a respective deadline. You should not leave tasks open ended and incomplete for a long period of time. When you are asked to do something, just do it. Don't put yourself in a position that could lead you to embarrassment, or worst, termination. So just set attainable goals with a deadline to ensure that you finish a task. You want to achieve your goals and become successful.

Events

Administrators are a very key component in orchestrating a company's event. The events can be small such as office celebrations or on a larger scale such as conferences. Whatever the event, we have to be involved and ready. Having structure and prioritizing event tasks are essential to our responsibilities to make sure we don't leave anything out. This is when your project management skills come into play.

Creating a specific project list for an event can help you prioritize what comes first. It keeps you on schedule and in some instances ahead of schedule. Let me give you an example. My organization has an annual conference that is huge and very important. It has a lot of moving parts, meaning that there are a lot of people and variables involved that I must maintain.

I must maintain and monitor this event schedule because it is imperative in order to have a successful outcome. I outline and list all the areas that are involved in the event so I can schedule times for certain tasks to be done or completed. The appropriate person is also assigned to complete a specific task. I don't micromanage this project. I simply check in on the separate entities involved, make sure they are on schedule, provide any resource assistance that they

may need and answer any questions they may have. They are the subject matter experts in their respective fields. Not me. They provide me

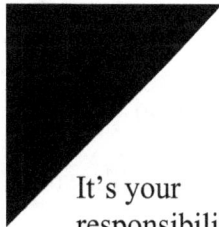

It's your responsibility to make sure everything is always taken care of and there are no outstanding items that need to be addressed.

with what's needed, and I'll tell them what's expected. It is called teamwork. My primary responsibility is to structure the skeleton of the event and they provide the meat. Working together as a team with an itemized and timely schedule, makes for a successful event each year.

The Follow Up

After you have organized your tasks, managed your teams, and completed assignments, you want to always follow up with any pending items. It's your responsibility to make sure everything is always taken care of and there are no outstanding items that need to be addressed. You must check in with everyone involved, ask questions and maybe even do some troubleshooting for them. The ultimate goal is for whatever assignment you are given to be completed successfully in a timely manner. Don't think that any task is too minor to address.

Sometimes the smallest items can cause the largest issues. Please do yourself a favor and follow up with everyone and everything. It will save you plenty of embarrassment later.

Hosting a team meeting in person or on a conference call is always a great way to make sure things are happening according to plan. This allows everyone to update each other and allow the team to possibly provide support in each other's areas. Two minds are always better than one. So welcome others to provide ideas, suggestions, and feedback to the project at hand. Just make sure you have a set agenda with a specific meeting goal as your foundation to prevent conversations from getting offline. You need to be the spearhead of the meeting. You are the only one that knows all parts and parties involved. So be confident, come prepared and be willing to receive information from others. Remember you can't do it all. The more positive help the better for you and the organization.

Take a lot of notes so that you know what needs to become action items for the next meeting. This makes it much easier for you to follow up with someone or something after the meeting. When multiple people meet, so much can happen that you don't want to lose. There is a lot of brainstorming of ideas, thoughts, new tasks and more that come about in meetings. To think that you can remember all of that is ridiculous. Remember from earlier in this book, it's perfectly fine to ask someone else who is better at note taking to record what's needed. Or you can always record the meetings and refer to them later. Whatever method you use, just make sure it gets done. You have to align everything all together and make sure that it all is successful.

Chapter 7

Toolbox

There are certain must-have qualities that a person in this role must possess in order to function effectively. These are things that cannot be taught, only developed.

Confidence in Yourself

In this book, I have talked about many physical tools and resources you can use to make your job more efficient. Tools that you can buy,

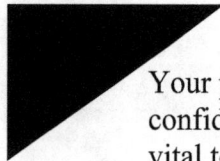

Your personal confidence is vital to your personal and professional success.

download, or operate daily to get specific tasks completed. But to be honest, there is one amazing resource that is extremely important that I haven't referenced a lot. All of the resources and tools wouldn't even be possible to use without it. It's crucial to the overall success of this position and the perception of the organization. That resource is you. You are the essential component to this seat. Everything revolves around and involves you in great detail. Your knowledge, your skills, your strategies, your ideas drives the vehicle that carries the entire organizational needs. You are the central force, or what I like to call, information central. Every department, employee, guest, vendor, or community liaison must connect with you at some point to get a mission accomplished or question answered. This is because you serve, know, support, protect and respect your leader. You are great. But you must first understand that and believe it to be true.

Your personal confidence is vital to your personal and professional success. Confidence helps you face tasks and ultimately complete them. When you are confident, you immediately know that you can get this done and get it done right. You believe in yourself and your abilities. You know what you master and what you may have a challenge with doing. And when you have confidence in yourself, challenges are not hard to face. You seek out strategies, alternatives or even help to get it done. Without that self-assurance, you may make unnecessary mistakes and fall behind in completing something because you don't want to be honest in what you don't know. Your confidence in yourself and your abilities is very important. It's a must have in this role.

If you are struggling with confidence, it's alright. First admit it and then figure out why it is a hindrance for you. Is it lack of education? First time in the position? Lack of understanding? Fear of failure? Whatever it is, you have to know it and work on it daily because rather you are in this role or another, how you feel about yourself or what you think about you is vital to your overall well-being. My suggestion in tackling the situation would be talking to someone - a friend, mentor, or spouse. Choose someone you can trust and who won't use your vulnerability against you. This is not to spread your business all over the place. Talking to someone and getting your reservations out of your head can help a great deal. It frees your mind from tackling this thing alone and breaks down the fear that no one understands. It also can provide some peace in getting everything off of your chest, so to speak.

Another suggestion to building your confidence is to sharpen your skills. This is great for those who struggle with fear of knowledge and education. You can decide to find formal training in a specific area or research online. YouTube has so many free resources in an infinite amount of areas that you can try. There are online courses in technology, note taking, presentation techniques, effective communication, typing and more. You just have to know what you want to enhance and go for it. You can also search for an industry related mentor who can guide you through certain areas of concern for you. It's all up to you and how much you want to help yourself. The resources are there. You just have to dive in them. The more you know, the more confident you are in yourself. You will begin to become more self-sufficient and proactive in certain responsibilities. Determine what you need and go for it. It's worth the personal investment because developing strong confidence in yourself will only bring you much success.

Reliability and Dedication

My leader oftentimes shares weekly devotions with the staff during our meetings. They are rich with the scriptures, personal testimonies, and commentary that reminds us all of why we do what we do every day for our organization. It's great to learn from him and we have grown to expect it each and every week. One week we were discussing the change of leaders and people not being on their post where those who needed them can find them. And he said something that stuck with me. "No one can take your seat, unless you get up!" Wow, right? That says so much. Especially in reference to this position. Being present, dedicated, and reliable is so important in this role. We have to be there at all times unless there is a health concern or emergency. Our leaders and others in the organization depend on us. If we are the spine and don't show up for work, where does all of our parts get their direction from? What happens to everyone when we are not on our job? This is not a scenario we want to consider often.

Although one person should not be responsible for everything at all times, this seat is so important that it can be that way at times. We have gone through a good chunk of what we do daily in this book. But think about the things we didn't discuss. It's so much that comes across our desks that needs our attention at any moment that other people can't begin to understand. If we are not at our post ready to tackle everything, what happens to it all? That's why it's so important that we are always in position when possible. We have to be dedicated to serving our leaders and the organization. We must approach this position as if what we do is so extremely important to everyone, because it is. What we do is more than just what we can see. Supporting a leader of a high-level affects and impacts so many people and their families. Take responsibility and ownership of this role and treat it with the utmost respect. Be present and be great!

Relationship Building & Communication

In the support staff position, you encounter so many people daily. These can vary from other administrative assistants, celebrities, executives, and department managers. You even interact with other key organizational employees daily such as security, maintenance staff, and food vendors. These are people who also make the magic happen behind the scenes that add to the success of an organization. How you communicate and treat every one of these people is important. You want to treat everyone with the same respect that you want reciprocated. You don't want to have an unprofessional demeanor or rude communication with anyone. Your goal should always be to communicate in a professional and respectful manner. Your words and action should be of love and not hate. Remember you are a direct representation of your leader and the person most guests see first. You should always want to present yourself in a positive light amongst everyone you interact with.

Building relationships with your coworkers and

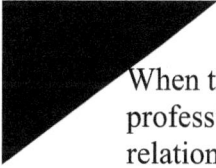

> When there is a professional relationship developed, the impossible can become possible right when you need it.

key staff members will be one of your greatest assets. You all should operate as a team. There will be a time when you all need each other. And you may need them to perform a favor or an out-of-the-normal request for you to make something happen. This is more easily accomplished when you have been respectful and polite to them every day. When there is a professional relationship developed, the impossible can become possible right when you need it. Creating an environment of negativity and division can hurt not only your organization, but yourself as well. Be the change agent. Set a warm and comfortable environment where relationships are nurtured and respect for all is

expected. It will benefit you more than you could
imagine.

Chapter 8

Poker Face

This position requires you to have thick skin. You cannot allow everything said and done to affect you. And everything that affects you can't be said openly. You have to learn how to respond at the right time in the right place. You don't want to be a doormat. But don't sit in the spirit of offense so long where you become unprofessional.

Professional Correspondence

I'll be honest with you in saying this concept is still a challenge for me. It's hard for me to maintain thick skin but it's so absolutely needed in this role. We interact with people of all walks of life that are coming with various unfriendly personalities. And in this role, you have to treat everyone with respect even if they don't give it to you.

So, maintaining your cool is an ability you must continuously develop in this specific role. Your job literally depends on it. This is such a challenge for me that I took a personality assessment to gain more insight about myself. I wanted to see what my personality type was and to understand other personalities as well. It helped me learn that I can handle this job with all the various difficulties that come along with it, including people. The personality test helped me understand that everyone is not like me, I can't control them, but I can control how I respond to others. And that is key in any position held that deals with the public.

Right Time, Right Place

Sometimes your leader can communicate with you in a nice way and sometimes they communicate in a not-so-nice way. Instructions can seem like a directive, command, or request that may take you by surprise. It's literally the nature of the position and you can't take it personal. Those not-so-friendly or sharp requests are not against you as a person in most cases. It's just clearly your leader responding to a deadline approaching, pressured opportunity, or just their personal bad day. Is it fair that this happens? No. But it does. And when it does you have to always be the bigger person and respond appropriately. Your response will determine what happens next in any situation. This is not easy to do but it's necessary if you care about your position. One thing I recommend keeping in your mind is this old cliché phrase, "Don't

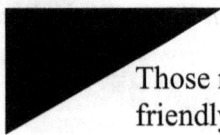

Those not-so-friendly or sharp requests are not against you as a person in most cases.

take it personal, it's just business." People do things and say things to get a rise out of you in any environment. Pass the test with a smile and not with what you really want to say.

Don't take it personal is the best advice I have for handling people that don't communicate with you well. That's a problem within themselves that they must handle. What you must do is approach every situation in a professional manner and deal with those situations head on. The mature thing to do is deal with it and move on. Always remember this is your work and not your life. After a certain time of the day, you don't even have to be around people. In a few hours, you will be in a place that truly matters to you and deserves you being present at that time. That place is home. We just need to do what we have to in order to get through the day. We all want the day to be wonderful and where everything is pleasant. But depending on where you work and who you work with, that isn't always possible.

The ideal work environment would be one that is happy and where everyone is courteous. And some places are actually like that. I have served numerous leaders who were easy to communicate with and very approachable. If there was something they were happy with, I was praised. If it was something they weren't pleased with, they invested the time to correct it with me, which provided me the opportunity to excel the next time. These were the ideal places to grow and learn more about what I truly wanted to accomplish professionally. But then there are other places where the leader is always mad, employees are uncomfortable and there is no interest in your professional growth. All that is expected is productivity and results. You have to know where you are and what matches your personality. Every work environment isn't for everyone. And every work environment isn't meant to be your last. But regardless of what the environment is, if you are there, be your best and respond to others respectfully.

Remain at Peace

When responding to negativity in a professional manner, the first thing is to stay calm. Having confidence in knowing that this bad energy isn't caused by you, nor is it personal to you, should help you remain in a peaceful position. Staying calm can help you understand the real issue that needs to be addressed and give you time to digest all that is being thrown your way. When you are calm, it's easier to remain respectful in difficult times because you are the level-headed one in the situation. Understand that effectively reacting to a negative behavior is a learned skill. It won't always be easy at first. But with time it will get better. If initially you feel this just won't happen, please refrain from saying anything. Just remain silent until you can articulate yourself well.

Your communication has to be very tactful with your leader and others. In intense situations, your response can counteract the negativity that is happening. When you stand your position and remain respectful, it can show the other person just how ridiculous they are behaving. Your peace can ultimately change the atmosphere. Having that thick skin and carrying yourself with confidence can help eliminate a bad interaction. Being an excellent communicator with interpersonal skills can minimize a lot. Allow your graceful presence to go before you and speak on your behalf even when you don't say a word. You never want to respond in a

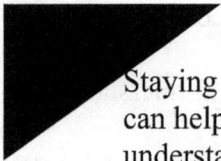

Staying calm can help you understand the real issue that needs to be addressed and give you time to digest all that is being thrown your way.

combative manner that can come across as insubordination. That would not be good. However, don't allow anyone to disrespect you by trying to tear you down with words either. So, when the right time comes later, feel confident enough to speak with your leader and let them know how you feel. This may work and it may not. It all depends on your demeanor, timing, and approach, as well as their honesty and response.

You don't have to keep taking things and being abused by anyone, especially your leader. No one has to endure verbal abuse for a paycheck. I've learned that sometimes bosses don't really know the best way to or know the most effective way to communicate to someone in a respectful manner. Sometimes they lack that skillset of effective communication, in which case that will be your decision if you want to continue to work for them. That's a choice that you would have to make but you have to know yourself and what you are worth. I personally choose to work in an environment where I'm respected and valued in many ways. Oftentimes you're not going to be valued in every way that you desire, but self-respect is more valuable than anything else. Sometimes it's easy to get respect when given and other times it's not. Either way, respect yourself first and every good decision will be easier to make after that.

Knowing Who You Are

Respect is huge in any relationship, not just professional. In some environments, disrespect starts to rear its ugly head when professional lines have been crossed. What I mean by this is there becomes a misunderstanding of who you are and what you are there to do. Your leader is not looking for a relationship, a friendship, or a partnership, they are looking for a team who will assist with making their job easier. When you recognize and clearly understand this, it won't seem so hurtful when your leader may communicate in an unfriendly manner. When this happens, you will respond and react in a more professional manner because your emotions are not involved. Always remember, when interacting with your leader keep your interaction specific to the task or situation. You can be friendly and courteous but get

Your leader is not looking for a relationship, a friendship, or a partnership, they are looking for a team who will assist with making their job easier.

right to the point. Executives usually don't have a lot of time to allocate to the admins, anyway, so be respectful of their time. Provide them with what they need, ask if there is anything else, provide solutions to problems and move on. Try not to linger in their office

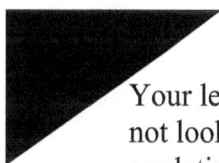

space or try to hold small talk. That's what you do with your friends, not your boss.

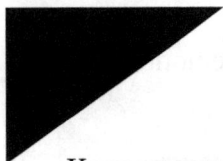

> Keep your personal life separate from your professional life to be on the safe side.

Keeping your lines clear with your leader will help you in many ways. For one, the respect level will be different as discussed previously. When you receive a performance review or evaluation, it will be easier to accept the outcome. You can take feedback and criticism more constructively when your lines are clear, versus personally when they are not. It's easy to fall into a pattern or routine of being more than you should be to your leader. Especially if they are nice and loves to communicate. But always keep in mind that this relationship is professional. Your work is your work and your friends are your friends. Keep your personal life separate from your professional life to be on the safe side. This will help you and cause you to develop boundaries to keep yourself free of disappointment, hurt, and disrespect from your leader.

Facial Expressions

My facial expressions say what I'm thinking almost all the time! I try my best to keep a poker face but sometimes it's so hard. I forget most times and someone else will remind me of my expression, so I can correct it immediately. Although this is an area that I haven't quite mastered yet, I want you to be better than me. Whatever words you don't say with your mouth, can show on your face if you don't control it. And sometimes what you don't say is far worse than what you would. It's very important to be mindful of your facial expressions at work. This includes smirking, frowning, or rolling your eyes. If something is said that you disapprove of or something that was said that was offensive to someone else, you want to be mindful of your facial expressions – understanding that they can tell your position on the topic. Unless your position is neutral, refraining from showing it on your face is best. Trust me, this is a hard thing to do but we can do it.

Our goal is to always exhibit a pleasant and professional demeanor at all times. We want to remain approachable to everyone, so our facial expressions have to display that. We don't want people assuming they know our emotions or that we have passed judgment on them. So please monitor your facial and what it says on your behalf.

Body Language

As we talked about non-verbal communication in a previous chapter, let's go more in-depth here. Another form of communication to remember is the language your body speaks. The way you stand, hold your arms, and lean in or away from someone, says it all in most cases. And maintaining a positive body language is also very critical in the workplace as well. For instance, if you are engaged in a conversation with someone and your arms are folded, that gives off the notion that you are guarded. It says you are on defense and feel the need to protect yourself from something or someone. If you happen to be in a meeting and you're folding your arms, it can sometimes convey negativity or frustration. These are definitely vibes you do not want to give off in a business setting. Try to maintain a calm, peaceful, and assertive posture during work at all times - especially when you are having a discussion or meeting with your leader. You want them to think you are listening, so use eye contact. You want them to feel you are engaged, so stand or sit up straight. And you want them to feel that you are paying attention, so keep your head up.

These are just some simple body language tips to remember when you are at work that can help you give a good impression.

Some additional ones that are really important is to stay away from seductive body language in a professional setting. Don't constantly touch yourself or others in public. Keep your hands in areas that can be easily seen when speaking to another coworker. You never want to come off provocative which can divert attention away from your true skills and abilities. This also is true for your attire. Make sure that your clothing is appropriate and not drawing attention to specific areas of your body if possible. You want to make sure people are engaging in a conversation with you because they value your opinion and not your physical attributes. One last helpful hint is to monitor your tone of voice as well. Try to speak at a very monotone level, staying away from whispering or high-toned pitches. Stay clear of any misleading physical gestures that can present an untrue picture of yourself.

Stressful Situations

Over the years I have learned that being able to handle stressful situations comes with maturity. This maturity can be in the age of the person or the years of work-related experience someone possesses. Either way, it's a needed skill when you are in a role of the administrative support staff field, which changes at any moment. You have to know how to keep your composure and not get frazzled when things are not going as planned. You need a calm disposition in order to figure out how to fix something that has gone wrong. Allow me to give you a personal example. My executive was traveling internationally and needed specific documents for his travel. I was unaware of this process, but I got it done in time. The issue came into play when he got to the airport. The documents I submitted were correct, but I entered his name into the visa portal incorrectly. I had his first name as his last name, and his last name as his first name. Because of this, he could not board his flight. This delayed his travel several hours, which when you travel internationally can prevent you from getting to your destination because of the connecting flight schedules. And that's exactly what happened.

My leader had to be rerouted to a different city and catch another flight a day later. This made him miss a day of his travel plans. This was extremely difficult to handle. I had to fix this situation as best I could without losing it completely. From home, I was responsible for correcting the document, changing his flights and getting him to his conference. I did just that without fumbling but it didn't feel good. I couldn't do anything but be honest and finish my assignment.

Owning the truth in stressful situations is always best. It helps you get through a tough time and you sleep better at night. I would rather be truthful about it than to lie about it because eventually the truth will prevail. The truth will come out, so I don't want to be caught in a situation where I've been found to lie. That is never my preference or an option for me. It should not be for you either.

Another situation where it became stressful was when there was some fraudulent activity happening. It wasn't immediately detected but over time I was able to know that something wasn't right. My executive once again was scheduled to travel internationally, and some money was requested for travel documentation. The correspondence that was submitted was standard like always for an engagement request. Things were moving along as usual without any indication of fraud. It wasn't until the agency started requesting additional funds in order to expedite our process, which I started looking into it more closely. I researched it and the information along with the fees that were requested was correct. All of that was cleared and appeared to be correct. So, I proceeded with two payment requests until the third request appeared. After further probing, I learned that this agency was an imposter. They used factual information in an attempt to extort money out of us. Although I was able to finally figure it out, I had already made two payments which totaled a small amount (less than a thousand dollars). This was a financial loss for us and an embarrassment for me since I had to be the one to inform my leader of this false invite situation.

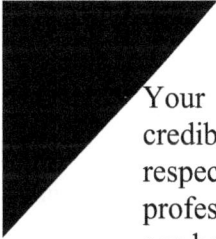

Your credibility and respect as a professional can be challenged and put to the test. But honesty and integrity will always outweigh anything else.

This situation took me some time to handle and I had to get my legal department involved as well. It was a lot to handle and very stressful. Especially after all of the details came out. A situation involving fraud had never occurred before in my role working as an executive assistant. It was very stressful and hard to deal with it but again, I told the truth while working through it. Mistakes like these happen and everyone is not going to handle them the right way. But as long as you remain calm and do what's right to fix it, that's what's most important. Your credibility and respect as a professional can be challenged and put to the test. But honesty and integrity will always outweigh anything else. Do your best and everything else will fall into place after that. It may overwhelm you initially, but it will all work out in the end. Just stay calm, focused, and honest.

Chapter 9

Beauty in Obedience

This role carries a special anointing. It is the ultimate honor and privileged to serve the Kingdom from the front seat. It can be strenuous and overwhelming at times. But when it is done in excellence and efficiency, there are tremendous blessings given to you.

The People You Meet

My goodness! Being in this role I have been blessed to meet some incredible people. You are the right hand of some great people that you support. When they are in great company, many times so are you. This is all dependent upon if your leader is influential in their field such as a pastor, a dignitary, government official, or some type of senior executive. No matter the capacity of who you are assisting, you may get to meet the people that they know. These are incredible people that you normally would not have met had you not known or been in this position. The opportunities afforded can be tremendous in so many ways. Meeting distinguished people can aid you in finding answers to life's questions just by being in their presence. You can find avenues or access to things that you may have been pondering. You get a chance to network with high-level or even famous people. These opportunities don't just come; they multiply over time depending on who your leader is to society or in society. This not only depends on your leader, but it also depends on the level of excellence and professionalism you possess and provide. When you are an excellent and trustworthy admin, your name will be called, and you will be brought into great company. This is because *your reward is in your work.* Treasure what you do, and treasure will come to you in many different ways.

There is beauty in your obedience. For instance, I have been blessed to meet Oprah, President Obama, President George Bush, Johnny Depp, and even Lady Gaga. I had these great opportunities because of whom I was associated with and the great organization where I was employed. Sometimes the opportunity isn't just for you to be blessed but to also bless other people. For instance, I was able to meet gospel singers Mary Mary, and minister directly to Tina. At that time Tina was experiencing a very public infidelity situation within her marriage and God gave me a prophetic word just for her. I would have never been in that space to bless that wonderful woman if it wasn't for my position. And I will never forget it.

Being an executive assistant, has given me the chance to meet celebrities but also some very influential people in corporate America as well. As an assistant for many years in the financial industry, I was often responsible for setting up events, planning conferences, and more high-level networking events. I've flown to different states every month performing as the main project manager for my company, which came with a lot of responsibility. I had to meet with other financial companies, high executives and key players from all over the world to ensure that everything from the agenda to the expenditures were all taken care of for everyone. This amount of work and level of responsibility was tremendous. It placed me in the company of so many people whose names may not be recognizable, but their net worth and company influence was known worldwide.

My company executives trusted me to be in such great company because of my work ethic and professionalism. Because my performance in house was on a level of excellence, I was trusted to perform the same way in other settings and environments. I was respectful, able to communicate effectively, my appearance was professional, and I carried myself in a confident manner. These are all the things I have been discussing with you through this entire book that have blessed me. And it will surely do the same for you. It will place you in scenarios and places you couldn't even imagine. It can fast track your work experience and elevate your level of influence. These opportunities will come to you often when you receive positive feedback on something you have done. When you embrace your position, don't take everything personal and develop confidence in yourself, opportunities to meet incredible people will be endless.

Divine Connections

When you speak of a spiritual meaning to what you are doing, divine connections are key. These are people and resources that have been orchestrated by God to make sure everything comes into play. You don't have to be in a church environment like myself, to experience a divine connection. You can be anywhere doing anything, and it could happen. The key is that you are doing what God has intended for you and were in the right place at the right time. In his right time, he takes care of your next step or next assignment by connecting you to the right person or group of people. It will all make sense or unveil over time. I believe strongly in divine assignments and purpose. And that's when divine connections happen. When God wants something to happen for you, and because it's your turn, your season, your time, and for a blessing, He will work everything out for your good. I personally don't do anything without knowing the purpose for it. I make a conscious effort to seek God in everything I do. And He always leads me in the right direction. Proverbs 3:5-6 states: *Trust in the Lord will all thine heart; and lean not unto thine own understanding. In all thy ways acknowledge him, and he shall direct thy paths.*

In thinking about a divine connection, it states that something here is supposed to happen and that there is purpose and reasons for it. He can speak to you through another person that can impact you more than you could have imagined. Divine purpose isn't just for you but to be used to help so many others. His message or connection may be small, but its purpose is infinitely extensive. It's more than you and it's bigger than you. And you experience such a thing when you are where you are supposed to be, doing what you are supposed to do. Do not look at your position as just something to pass time. There is always something divine in everything that is done with a pure heart. Out of your obedience, God could elevate you to your next level or give you directions for your new assignment. But you have to be in position, have an open heart, and be ready to receive what God is saying. Staying divinely connected keeps you always in alignment with His purpose. Everything is all God. He engages the Holy Spirit, Jesus, and all of His angels just for you when you are ready. Pay attention and be prepared.

Unusual Resources and Assistance

This role does carry a special anointing. We know ultimately that God is our source. And through that source, our instruments, and resources needed shall be supplied, and most commonly through people.

In this role, you have a tremendous amount of access that the general population does not. For instance, you may have access to certain clubs or private facilities, and you may have special privileges into places and to people that can benefit you professionally and personally. Whatever it is, it's generally unusual or not the norm. These are resources that are not organically yours but because of the people you support, it's almost a given to you as well.

Allow me to give you an example. God allowed me to divinely connect with a young woman at my work environment that has blessed me so much. God led her to me one day based on something I said one day that moved her. We started talking and she began to speak into my life about the story that was within me to even write this book. Then God touched her heart to want to work with me by providing easy resources that she had access to. She had a plethora of information, skills, and abilities that was unusual to me for a few reasons. One, because based on what she does at the office, I would not have known all that she does outside of it that have benefited me. And for two, God divinely connected her to me to bless me with encouragement and support that I needed to get my assignment of completing this book accomplished.

She is my unusual resource for so many things and I am thankful for her truly.

Leadership Training

When you think of your leader, there is an enormous amount of power and authority that comes with their position. In the ministry world, we say that there is a great anointing on a leader in order for them to do what they do daily. It's a ministry or calling from God. No matter if you serve a leader in the church or a Fortune 500 company, there is something special which keeps them at a certain altitude. There is a great responsibility to share or pass down that skillset to another person as well. No one can stay on top forever and nor should they want to. A great leader should always be preparing his replacement. The mantle of

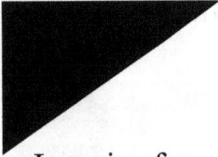

Learning from a great leader is a huge benefit for you. If your leader values you, they may consider investing in you.

greatness and the blessed spiritual oil that a leader possesses should be poured over a credible, reliable, and prepared successor. And that person could be you.

You want to always be paying enough attention to your leader to learn something positive from them. Even if they are not the nicest person, they have a certain skillset or anointing that can develop you. Learning from a great leader is a huge benefit for you. If your leader values you, they may consider investing in you. This time is valuable and could be preparing you for your next level. Don't take it for granted. Pay attention. Observe. Receive. And ask questions. Always be open to learning new things and in different ways. The revelation that you can receive from learning from another person can be life changing. You are in the direct seat to receive all of the oil, favor, grace, and anointing from the person who has it all. All you have to do is be present and want it. Others would love to have access to greatness like you do. God gave you this, right? He divinely chose you for this time and this place. Try to remember that and be prepared to receive something that can change your entire life.

Education & Training

Sitting in the role of supporting a great influential leader is an extreme educational opportunity. Why do I say this? I say this because it truly is just that. You don't have to attend a traditional college or university to be educated. Experience and opportunity outweigh formal education every time. Being in this role provides just that. The experiences I have had in supportive roles are just as great as the leader I serve and have served. The true education is being present, learning, and understanding what being taught. Understanding the who, what, when, where, why and how of your area or divine assignment.

Learn to understand the beginning to the end of a thing, its creation, and to its execution. Understand that the creator of what you're learning and why they wanted to create it. That's more valuable than anything you can read in a book. It's literally first-hand knowledge and great on-the-job training. I'm not against formal education. I'm a college graduate myself. But I am living proof that what I learned in a book may have got me through the door, but it was my knowledge and experience that kept me at the table.

You can't be afraid to educate yourself in this role. Just look in front of you and realize what you have access to. The simplest tasks may hold the greatest treasures. For example, in the role as an executive assistant or administrator, or secretary you are exposed to so much. You get to read board minutes in which you are learning the key corporate players and their specific roles. You get to review financial documents that teach you how organizations keep their records, manage, and disperse funds daily. Reviewing finances can also teach you what to and not to do in order to stay in business as well. You get to understand and learn about some of the in-house and external strategies companies and corporations use, and not-for-profit organizations may use to help run the organization. You are usually the first one to test out or review new products in technology and other advanced areas. You name it, you have access to it. It just all depends on how you are viewing your current responsibilities. When you look closely you will see that you have a front row seat that most individuals who are in college pay to learn about. Take advantage. Every lesson counts.

There really are not any excuses, in today's world of instant access, not to teach yourself. Once again, you can Google or YouTube just about anything you want to know. And when that isn't enough, you can attend classes online that can further sharpen your skills. You can get a mentor or shadow someone that is already doing what you want to do. The possibilities are endless. It's just about what you want to learn and when. Education is that acquired desire within to learn more about something. And then when you know more, you will be able to go to and teach others how to do it more effectively. Education and training is the greatest gift you can ever give someone. Take the time and invest in your own growth so you can be a blessing to someone else one day.

I read and study material that provides information, inspiration, revelation, transformation, and motivation. I want to know more, know why, and know how to use it. All of this coupled with my experience develops me into a great resource. That's why experience is such a great thing to have. Experience is learning something that you didn't know before and putting it to use firsthand. When you experience something, you can become the expert. You can teach and talk about it with conviction and with passion because you went through it. You can do it convincingly and with excitement. Let's use the example of divorce. If you are a divorcee, you can talk to someone who is going through divorce and support them emotionally because know you can relate to them better than someone who has not been through a divorce.

Experience can better represent a case more because it speaks to the reality and not an assumption. With experience comes conviction and passion. And with that, you can potentially persuade another person on whatever because you are a living witness. Education is good and experience is great. Education and experience together is powerful. Try it all and see what an amazing opportunity you can create for yourself.

Dreams Manifested

Serving in this role carries another type of

gifting. Serving in the Kingdom of God is an honor and privilege. The kingdom is amazing when you think about it. When you think of the word Kingdom, you think about kingship, rulers, queens, princesses, princes and more. You think of royalty. And that is exactly what it is, royalty, prestige, and an amazing experience. I know using the word Kingdom is taking the spiritual approach to this role, but that's intentional because everything we do is for God, or at least in my opinion, it should be. No matter what environment or industry you are working in, you want every assignment to be pleasing to the Lord. God created you with a natural and spiritual right to be whatever you want, everything you do is for Him. You have a right to be all that you can be in him and through Him. He provides you with the opportunities to meet incredible people, make divine connections, and you have an opportunity to receive oil directly from people who already possess great power in doing what you desire.

When you do anything with your whole heart and in excellence, there are blessings that come along with it just as a reward. This reward can be natural like money, cars, and houses. And this reward can be spiritual such as oil, anointing, and spiritual gifts. However, it is received, it is always great when it comes from God. As we may know from various Bible readings, the manifestation of great things comes through obedience. Obedience is *dutifully complying with the commands, orders or instructions of one in authority.* When you do what you are supposed to do, when you are supposed to do it, and be where you are supposed to be, the desires of your heart will come to pass. It's not like making a wish or bargaining with things that if you want this you have to do that. It's truly being with a pure heart doing those things that you are asked and required. Understanding and respecting authority. Helping those who are in need. Listening to His instructions. Obeying and doing all of those things can manifest dreams into reality.

Know that serving a person in an organization that you may not be too happy in, but it's in God's will, and can be very challenging to most to say the least. Especially if you are not looking at all things through a spiritual lens. But you have to be clear that everything you do, and experience isn't always for you at that moment. It could be to bless, teach, or help someone else. But in your obedience to do that very thing for someone else, God will bless you even more. Don't look at going to get coffee for a boss, or staying late to complete a project as hard work. Let it excite you that those things you are doing are through obedience to God, and not just your love and dedication to the Lord. Through that obedience, He will allow divine connections, present unusual resources, opened doors, expedited elevation, and so much more to push you ahead of the average. Because of your integrity in your work, your commitment and dedication, and professional manner, He will provide you access to privileges, experiences and favor beyond your comprehension. Your education and who you know will have nothing to do with it. It's the blessings that come along with your obedience.

Conclusion

The purpose of this book is to not only help those in our roles to be better prepared to handle this job, but it is also to bring awareness to what this role entails. It's probably more than you thought, and more than most people consider when they think of our line of work. It is often overlooked, frowned upon, and minimized. But in actuality, we are the glue that makes this entire job work together. We support the visionary of our organization so that he or she can continue being great at what they do. We develop the relationships internally and externally that helps support and executes our overall mission. We inform and assist the guests, customers, congregants who spread the word about what we do and how we make them feel when we do it. We are the *spine* of this great body that we serve. We send communication to every part of this organization on what needs to be done, when, where, why and how. It's us that do that. And it is truly important, needed, and necessary. So now that you know you are more than the coffee retriever, file keeper, copy maker, and phone caller - you can embrace that you are special and the success of everything is your special assignment. You are the *Spine of the Temple* (or organization) in which you serve. Serve it with a pure heart and for the glory of God because He is the one that appointed you and assigned you there. And He is the one that matters most.